Contents

Introduction

What is involved?

Comparing involves the process of making judgements about two or more objects, situations or events in terms of similarities or differences. These can arise from any sensory observations, and/or by making specific comparisons involving the language of numbers, size, weight, capacity or time.

Measuring involves the process of using units of non-standard or standard measures to establish a sense of size, weight, capacity or time in relation to quantity.

Developing the skills

Children's first experiences of making comparisons are developed as they become more aware of their surroundings. They begin to recognize similarities and differences in colours, shapes, textures, sounds and tastes. They also begin to recognize differences in sizes or amounts of objects.

By the time children reach four years of age, those of average ability and above are starting to verbalize their everyday comparisons and beginning to relate these to notions of measures and quantity.

Early Learning Goals

This book provides a programme that helps children towards achieving the following Early Learning Goals for mathematics identified by the Qualifications and Curriculum Authority. By the end of the Foundation Stage, children should be able to:

- count reliably up to 10 everyday objects
- recognize numerals 1 to 9
- use language such as 'more' or 'less', 'greater' or smaller', 'heavier' or 'lighter', to compare two numbers or quantities
- use language such as 'circle' or 'bigger', to describe the shape and size of solids and flat shapes
- use everyday words to describe position
- use developing mathematical ideas and methods to solve practical problems.

Baseline Assessment

All of the activities in this book are focused around developing skills in young children that will enable them to achieve elements of the Early Learning Goals in the six areas of learning by the time they are five years of age. This will enable them to confidently tackle the Baseline Assessment tasks that they will be expected to carry out when they enter reception classes in mainstream schools.

How to use this book

This book gives children the opportunity to make visual and direct comparisons, to carry out simple measuring tasks using non-standard units of length, weight, capacity and time, and to begin to learn how to tell the time using 'o'clock' times.

The activities are designed to be used according to the children's level of development. They include practical group and individual activities, games focusing on numbers from 5 to 10 and photocopiable sheets that are designed to help children consolidate their skills of counting and writing numbers. Where the photocopiable sheet is to be used by individual

Finding out what children know beforehand

You can assess children to find out what they already know by checking:
- how far a child can count objects correctly by touching them and saying the number
- how far a child can write numbers in a recognizable form
- whether a child knows the names of and can recognize the primary colours and shapes such as circles, squares and triangles
- whether a child can point to the group containing more/less of the same object, for example five and three toy cars
- whether a child can point to the biggest/ smallest or longest/shortest object when shown two similar objects side by side, such as a big and small book
- whether a child can say which they think is the heavier object when given two different objects to hold in each hand
- whether a child can point to the container that they think holds the most water when shown a jug and a cup.

These assessment suggestions are developmental and will not necessarily be appropriate for all children.

children and can be kept for assessment purposes, it is referred to as 'Individual recording'; where it is to be used by a group of children, it is called an 'Individual task'. All of the activities are adult-directed and require the presence and interaction of an adult. It is therefore important that the activities are incorporated in planning procedures and that adult helpers are pre-briefed about the activities and the preparation that they will require.

Home links

Each activity includes suggestions for how parents and carers can help their children at home. To involve the support of parents and carers, include information in your parent's booklet and provide guidance informally, through daily contact. If you are concerned about a child and wish parents and carers to help their child with a particular skill, share your ideas with them and invite their observations.

Progression

The book starts with children being introduced to recognizing similarities and differences in shapes or objects in relation to colour, size and different properties, such as objects that float or sink. They then make simple comparative judgements about objects such as more or less, heavier or lighter and bigger or smaller. Simple activities are presented for children to measure, count and compare using non-standard measuring units, including timing games and problem-solving activities such as cooking.

Finally, activities are presented for children to learn to read and record times to the hour (o'clock). There are also some activities that involve whole group participation such as ordering children from shortest to tallest and making a whole group pictogram to show hair colours.

Apple tree game

Learning objective
To use the language 'same' or 'different' when comparing two numbers or quantities.

Group size
Four to six children working with an adult.

What you need
A copy of the photocopiable sheet for each child; A4 card and paper; scissors (for adult use only); crayons or felt-tipped pens; glue; spreaders; a tray.

Preparation
For the game: make four copies of the photocopiable sheet onto card. Colour the trees green and the apples red, then laminate the sheets and cut them into individual cards.
For the individual recording: divide a piece of A4 paper into three columns – label one 'A tree', one 'Same' and one 'Different'. Make four copies of the photocopiable sheet, cut into individual apple trees and place in a tray.

What to do
Look at the different apple tree cards with the children. Hold up two cards at a time (with the same or different numbers of apples) and ask them to make comparisons.

Spread the cards out face down on a table. Ask each child to take turns to pick up a card and then turn another over. If the card they have turned is the same as their own they keep it to make a pair and take another, then the next child takes a turn. If the card is different, they replace the card and play moves on to the next child. The child with the most pairs of cards at the end of the game is the winner.

Individual recording
Give each child a copy of the prepared photocopiable sheet. Tell the children to choose an apple tree sheet from the tray, colour it in and paste it into the first column. Then ask them to find an apple tree that is the same, and one that is different to colour in and paste into the appropriate columns on the sheet.

Support
Spread the cards out face up. In turn for each child, identify a card and ask them to find one that is the same.

Extension
Play the game with the children turning over two cards each time. If the cards match, they keep the pair. If they do not, they are replaced and play passes on to the next child.

Assessment
Can the child count the numbers of apples on the trees and tell you if there are more or less? Can he recognize numbers of apples by sight? Can he match pairs of trees with the same number of apples?

Home links
Encourage parents and carers to play a version of the 'Apple tree game', using aces to fives in two packs of cards.

Apple tree game

Big or small?

Learning objective
To use language such as 'more' or 'less', 'bigger' or 'smaller' to compare two numbers or quantities.

Group size
Four to six children working with an adult.

What you need
The photocopiable sheet; two A4 sheets of paper; a tray; glue; spreaders; pencils; crayons or felt-tipped pens.

Preparation
Make five copies of the photocopiable sheet onto card. Colour the animals, then laminate the sheets and cut them into individual cards. Make another five copies of the sheet and cut them up into separate animal pictures. Place the pictures in a tray. Label the two sheets of A4 paper, 'Big' and 'Small'.

What to do
Hold up different animals from the set of cards and ask the children to say the name each time. Hold up two elephant cards (one big and one small elephant) and ask the children to point out similarities and differences between them. Repeat with the other animals.

Next, sit the children around the two sheets of paper labelled 'Big' and 'Small' and spread out the big and small elephant cards face up (use more big elephants than small elephants). Ask each child in turn to find a big or a small elephant and place it on the correct sheet of paper. Count the sets of elephants with the children and ask, 'Which set has more/less elephants?'. Repeat this with the lions and tigers using different numbers of big/small animals each time.

Individual task
Place the tray of animal pictures in the centre of a table and give each child a copy of the prepared 'Big or small' sheet. Ask each child to choose one type of animal (elephants, lions or tigers) and paste some big and small animal pictures in the correct section on the sheet.

Support
Make a copy of the photocopiable sheet for each child. Ask the children to colour the animals. Cut out the animals and ask them to paste each animal picture in the correct section on the 'Big' and 'Small' sheets.

Extension
Provide the children with a larger selection of big and small animal pictures to paste in the correct sections.

Assessment
Check whether the child can name the animals and sort the big and small animals correctly. Can she count the animals and write the numbers on the sheet correctly?

Home links
Ask parents and carers to give their children an assortment of adult and children's socks for them to sort.

Big or small

More or less?

Learning objectives

To use the language 'more' or 'less', 'most' or least' when comparing two numbers or quantities; to recognize greater and smaller quantities.

Group size

Four to six children working with an adult.

What you need

A copy of the photocopiable sheet for each child; a piece of A4 paper for each child and one for yourself; a set of teddy counters or small countable objects in a tray; scissors; crayons or felt-tipped pens; glue; spreaders.

Preparation

Cut off the strip of teddies from each photocopiable sheet.

What to do

Place the tray of teddy counters in the centre of a table and give each child a sheet of paper. Put a small number of teddy counters on your sheet of paper and count them with the children. Invite the children to put a higher number of teddies on their own sheets of paper and count them together. Ask, 'Who used the most teddies?'. Repeat the activity, changing the number of teddies used. Invite the children to put less teddies on their paper. Ask, 'Who used the smallest number of teddies?'.

Individual recording

Ask the children to cut up their strip of teddies into individual cards. Invite them to paste four teddies into the first section on their photocopiable sheet and then paste a set containing more teddies into the second section. Ask them to colour one set in red and one in green, then to write how many are in each set in the boxes. Repeat with less teddies in the second section.

Support

Ask the children to paste two teddies in the first section and a set with one more teddy in the second section.

Extension

Ask the children, 'How many teddies are there altogether?', 'How many more red teddies are needed to make the number the same as the green teddies?' and so on.

Assessment

Check whether the child can make a set of teddies that is more or less than a given number. Note whether he counts the teddies in his head or by pointing to each one. Check that he writes the numbers on the sheet correctly.

Home links

Invite parents and carers to carry out a similar activity at home using saucers and small objects.

More or less?

Sink or float?

Learning objective
To use developing mathematical ideas and methods to solve practical problems.

Group size
Four to six children working with an adult.

What you need
A copy of the photocopiable sheet; one of each of the 12 objects drawn on the sheet; a large sheet of paper; a washing-up bowl filled with water; aprons; adult scissors; glue; spreaders.

Preparation
On a large sheet of paper, draw a line vertically and label each side 'Float' and 'Sink'. Cut the photocopiable sheet into individual pictures and place them in a tray.

What to do
Tell the children that they will be putting some objects into water to find out whether they float or sink. Ask the children if they can name anything that floats, and anything that sinks.

Talk about why objects float or sink in water. Explain that objects float if they are lighter than water and that heavy objects, such as boats, will float in water because they are filled with air and sealed to stop the water getting in.

Individual task
Ask each child to take a turn to place an object in the bowl to see whether it will float or sink, then to find the picture of the object in the tray and paste it to the correct side of the chart.

When they have finished, encourage the children to count the objects in each column on the chart with you. Write the number in each column and ask, 'Which set has more numbers of objects?'.

Support
Help the children to find the picture to match the object and paste it onto the chart.

Extension
Encourage the children to find other objects that float or sink and then draw them on the chart.

Assessment
Check that the child can say whether an object floats or sinks and can place the pictures of the objects in the correct column. When asked to compare the number of objects, can she identify the set with more objects?

Home links
Ask parents and carers to test with their children whether objects sink or float in the bath.

Sink or float?

boat	pebble	model car
plastic tub	2p coin	scissors
metal spoon	leaf	lolly stick
wooden brick	pencil	cork

Size matters

Learning objectives
To use the language 'taller than', 'shorter than', 'big', 'middle-sized' and 'small' when comparing different sizes of objects; to use everyday words to describe position.

Group size
Four to six children working with an adult.

What you need
A version of the traditional story of 'Goldilocks and the Three Bears'; a copy of the photocopiable sheet for each child; scissors; sheets of plain paper; glue; spreaders; crayons or felt-tipped pens.

What to do
Read the story of 'Goldilocks and the Three Bears' with the children joining in, using different voices for each bear. Explain to the children that they are going to stand in a line in height order from tallest to shortest. Invite two children to stand side by side in front of the group. Ask, 'Who is the taller/shorter child?'. Choose another child to join the line. Ask the group to look at this child and decide whether he or she is taller or shorter than the other children and whether he or she should stand

beside them or in between them. Repeat until all the children are standing in line.

Individual recording
Give each child a copy of the photocopiable sheet and a sheet of paper. Ask them to colour in and cut out the bears, chairs and beds and paste each set in size order, largest to smallest, on the sheet on paper.

Support
Cut out the pictures of bears, chairs and beds and place a set in a margarine tub for each child to sort.

Extension
Provide the children with four or more different-sized teddy bears or dolls to order in size from smallest to largest.

Assessment
Note whether the child can use the appropriate language and order the objects by size correctly.

Home links
Encourage parents and carers to help their children to draw a picture of their family in order of size.

Size matters

Longer or shorter?

Learning objective
To identify 'longer' or 'shorter' lengths of paper by sight.

Group size
Four to six children working with an adult.

What you need
A copy of the photocopiable sheet for each child; sheets of different-coloured A4 paper; a tray; glue; spreaders.

Preparation
Cut the coloured paper into strips, approximately 2cm wide, then into different lengths between 5cm and 25cm. Place the strips of paper in a tray.

What to do
Sit the children in a semicircle and lay a coloured strip on the floor. Invite each child in turn to choose a strip from the tray and lay it alongside the one on the floor. Ask the child, 'Is your strip longer or shorter than the first strip?'.

Encourage the children to rearrange the strips into size order, longest to shortest. Ask them to point out the strip nearest to the middle and tell them that this strip is 'middle-sized'.

Individual recording
Place the tray of strips of paper on a table (provide extra strips of approximately 5cm and 25cm) and give each child a copy of the photocopiable sheet. Ask them to colour in the strip in the middle of the sheet. Then, encourage them to find and paste a longer coloured strip of paper in the top part of the sheet and a shorter strip in the bottom part.

Support
Help the children to paste the longer and shorter strips in the correct places on the sheet.

Extension
Let the children use the back of the photocopiable sheet to paste a long strip at the top and a short one at the bottom, then find a middle-sized strip to paste in between them.

Assessment
Note whether the child can use the appropriate language and place the strips of paper in the correct size order.

Home links
Ask parents and carers to provide their children with a sheet of paper with two sections labelled 'longer' and 'shorter', and to encourage them to draw and colour pictures of objects longer or shorter than their hand. Ask parents and carers to print the name of each object.

Longer or shorter?

longer			shorter

Heavier or lighter?

Learning objective
To sort items into sets of 'heavier' and 'lighter' than a given object.

Group size
Four to six children working with an adult.

What you need
A copy of the photocopiable sheet for each child; a medium-sized potato; a pan balance; a tray of 12 different objects that are heavier or lighter than the potato (use a different number of heavier objects than lighter objects, for example, six heavier and four lighter); two large paper circles labelled 'heavier' and 'lighter'.

What to do
Using the pan balance, show the children what happens when one object is heavier and one is lighter, and when two objects are the same weight. Ask them to select an object from the tray and to take turns to balance their object against the potato. Encourage each child to say whether the object is heavier or lighter and then to place it in the correct labelled circle.

When all the objects have been balanced against the potato, ask the children, 'Are there more or less heavier objects than lighter objects?'. This can be repeated in another session by using a different item for the children to balance objects against.

Individual task
Give each child a copy of the photocopiable sheet. Ask them to choose three objects that are heavier than the potato and three that are lighter, and then to draw a picture of each in the correct circle.

Support
Ask the children to select and draw on the sheet one object that is heavier than the potato, and one that is lighter.

Extension
Encourage the children to find some different objects in the room to balance against the potato. Draw the objects in the appropriate circles on the photocopiable sheet. Ask, 'Are there more, less or the same number of heavier objects than lighter objects?'.

Assessment
Check whether the child understands how a pan balance works. Does she use the appropriate language when comparing the weight of objects? Does she draw the objects on the correct side of the sheet?

Home links
Ask parents and carers to use weighing scales with their children to balance different objects, and to write their findings down.

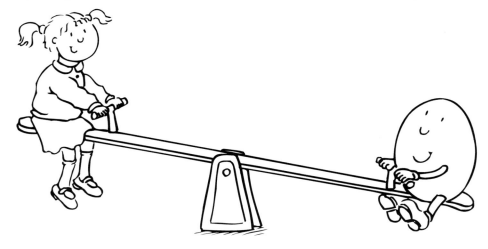

Heavier or lighter?

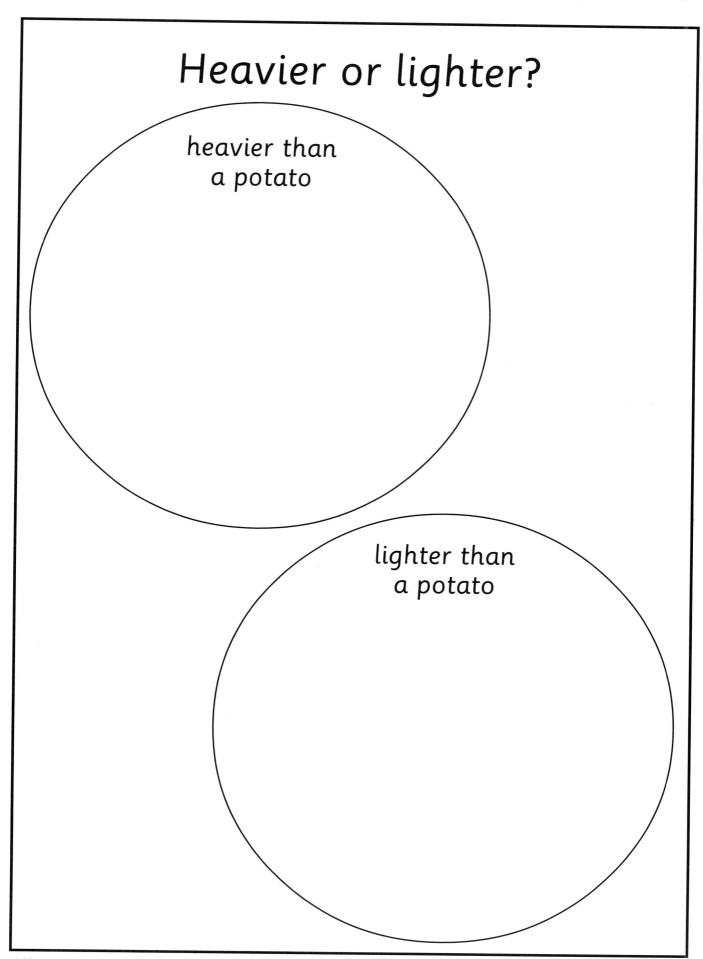

heavier than
a potato

lighter than
a potato

Pace it out!

Learning objective
To count reliably the number of paces to a given point and compare distances.

Group size
Four to six children working with an adult.

What you need
A copy of the photocopiable sheet for each child and one copy enlarged to A3 size; pencils; red, blue and black marker pens; flip chart.

Preparation
Make a copy of the photocopiable sheet and write in the names of five easily accessible places in the room, for example, the door or the window. Make further copies of the sheet for each child and attach an enlarged copy to the flip chart.

What to do
Make a starting line on the floor with a piece of rope or string and demonstrate to the children

how to pace slowly and count the steps. Then ask each child in turn to walk slowly while everyone counts his or her paces from the starting line to a place named on the chart.

After each turn, use a black marker to scribe the number of paces taken in the box on the enlarged photocopiable sheet.

Individual recording
Point to and say the name of each place on the flip chart and ask the children to tell you the number of paces they had to make. Ask, 'Which was the furthest/nearest place to walk to?'.

Invite the children to copy down the correct number of paces on their photocopiable sheet in the box beside the item. They should then draw a red circle around the number of paces that shows the furthest distance walked and a blue circle around the number of paces showing the nearest distance walked.

Support
Scribe the numbers in yellow in the boxes for children to trace.

Extension
Encourage the children to count their own paces to all of the places and to add the number to the photocopiable sheet each time. Talk about the possibility of some paces being longer than others. Demonstrate this by showing the children the difference between the length of your pace and a child's pace.

Assessment
Note whether the child can pace and keep track of the count correctly. Check whether he uses the appropriate language when comparing the distances walked. Can he write the numbers correctly on the sheet?

Home links
Encourage parents and carers to set pacing tasks for their children such as, 'How many paces from the front door to the kitchen door?.'

Pace it out!

To the _____ [ ] paces

To the _____ [ ] paces

To the _____ [ ] paces

To the _____ [ ] paces

To the _____ [ ] paces

Counting cupfuls

Learning objectives
To count reliably up to ten everyday objects; to use developing mathematical ideas and methods to solve practical problems.

Group size
Four children working with an adult.

What you need
The photocopiable sheet; a large sheet of paper; flip chart; a water tray; a funnel; a cup and a set of five different plastic containers that hold more than a cupful of water; glue; spreaders; pencils; a black marker pen.

Preparation
Make between five and ten copies of the photocopiable sheet. Cut up the sheets into individual cup pictures and place them in a tray. Draw a chart on a large sheet of paper with three columns and write the headings 'Container', 'Cupfuls of water' and 'Total' at the top. List the name of the various containers in the first column.
    Make a copy of the chart onto A4 paper and copy one for each child. Place the resources on a table close to the water tray. Attach the chart to a flip chart where everyone can see it.

What to do
Fill the first container listed on the chart with water using a cup and a funnel, asking the children to count aloud with you each time you fill and pour a cup of water into the container. Paste that number of cup pictures under 'Cupfuls of water' on the sheet, count them and fill in the 'Total' column. Repeat with the other containers. Discuss with the children which containers held more/less.

Individual recording
Encourage the children to paste cup pictures onto their copy of the chart to match the number in each row on the chart, and then write in the totals.

Support
Write a heading such as, 'A jug holds 6 cupfuls' on the back of the photocopiable sheet. Ask the children to paste cup pictures on the sheet to match the number.

Extension
Ask the children to order the containers in a line starting with the one that holds the least cupfuls to the one that holds the most.

Assessment
Check whether the child can pour and count cupfuls of water to fill a container reasonably accurately and write the number correctly. Note whether she can compare the results of two containers and say which holds more or less.

Home links
Ask parents and carers to continue the activity at home in the kitchen sink.

Counting cupfuls

Balancing act

Learning objectives
To count reliably the number of items needed to balance a given object; to recognize numerals with the highest and lowest values.

Group size
Four children working with an adult.

What you need
The photocopiable sheet; a bucket balance; a medium-sized ball of play dough or Plasticine; five tubs of small objects for balancing; a large table area; a black marker pen; pencils; crayons or felt-tipped pens.

Preparation
Make a copy of the photocopiable sheet and print the name of each set of objects clearly in the corner of each box. Make a copy for each child and an enlarged copy as a teaching chart.

What to do
Count aloud with the children to see how many small objects it takes to balance the ball. Fill in the total on the chart. Choose a child to place the next set onto the scales, again counting with the children. Continue around the group, balancing and counting the objects until all the number boxes are filled in and each child has had a turn.

Individual recording
Give each child a copy of the photocopiable sheet and ask them to look at the chart. Ask them to draw the different number of items in the large boxes and to write the number in the small boxes. Invite them to draw a red circle around the largest number of items and a blue circle around the smallest number.

Support
Write the heading 'A ball balances' on the back of the photocopiable sheet. Ask the children to choose one of the items from the chart and to draw a picture to show how many of the items balanced the ball.

Extension
Encourage the children to find a different set of small objects in the room to balance the ball, then draw a picture of the result and write the number on the back of the photocopiable sheet.

Assessment
Note whether the child can balance the ball against a set of objects reasonably accurately and can count and write the number correctly. Note whether he can compare two sets of objects and say which has more or less. Can he identify the sets of objects with the largest and smallest number of objects?

Home links
Encourage parents and carers to use a set of scales with a dial to find out with their children how many pieces of a fruit or vegetable will weigh 500g or 1lb.

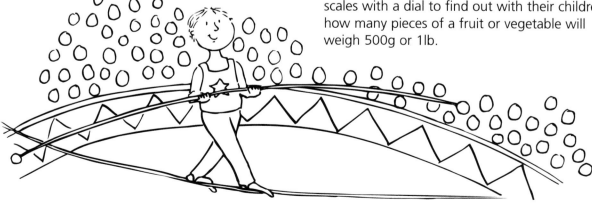

Balancing act

A ball balances

Points mean peppermints!

Learning objectives
To use developing mathematical ideas and methods to solve practical problems; to count reliably up to 12 everyday objects; to use language such as 'most' or 'least' when comparing sets of objects, and 'highest' or 'lowest' when comparing sets of scores.

Group size
Four children working with an adult.

What you need
For the peppermint creams: 500g ready-prepared royal icing; peppermint essence; green food colouring; icing sugar; small circular pastry cutters; petits fours cake papers; a large mixing bowl; small rolling-pins and pastry boards; plates. (**NB** Remember to check for any dietary requirements and food allergies.)
For the game: the photocopiable sheet; four sets of 12 coloured counters (one colour for each player); a spotty dice; a shaker; a margarine tub; flip chart.

Preparation
Make four copies of the photocopiable sheet onto card and laminate to make four playing boards. On a large sheet of paper, make a score sheet with five columns, on which you can fill in each child's name and their score for games one to four.

What to do
To make the peppermint creams, place the royal icing into the mixing bowl. Add a few drops of peppermint essence and green food colouring and knead into the icing. Give each child a rolling-pin, a pastry board, some cake papers and a plate. Dust each pastry board with icing sugar. Divide the mixture into four even balls and give one to each child. Ask them to roll out their mixture to a thickness of about 5mm, then cut out the sweets with the cutters. Place the sweets in cake papers and put them on a plate. Ask, 'Who made the largest/smallest number of sweets?' and 'Did anyone make the same number of sweets?'. Place the plates of sweets in the refrigerator to chill.

Individual task
Attach the score sheet to a flip chart where everyone can see it. Give each child a playing board and 12 counters. Explain that the children should take turns to throw the dice into the tub, then place that number of counters in a cake paper on the playing board. After everyone has had two throws, count the number of each child's counters with them and write their scores onto the flip chart. Ask, 'Who has the highest score?'. Draw a red circle around the winner's score. Repeat the game three times, then look at the score sheet to see who has had the highest score the most times. Invite the overall winner to choose a peppermint cream first, then share the rest between the group.

Support
Play the game with a dice or cube marked 1, 1, 2, 2, 3, 3.

Extension
Play the game using two dice and 24 counters for each child.

Assessment
Note whether the child can identify the plate with the largest/smallest and those with the same number when comparing the numbers of sweets, and the highest and lowest scores when playing the game.

Home links
Provide parents and carers with instructions for making peppermint creams at home.

Points mean peppermints!

Hair today

Learning objectives
To count different sets of items reliably; to use language 'more' or 'less', and 'most' or 'least' when comparing sets of items.

Group size
Whole class working with adults.

What you need
A copy of the photocopiable sheet for each child; four sheets of A3 paper; sticky tape; pencils; crayons or felt-tipped pens; scissors; glue; spreaders; ruler.

Preparation
Make a large wallchart from four A3 sheets of paper taped together with the heading 'Hair colours'. Give each sheet of paper a heading: 'Black', 'Brown', 'Red' and 'Blond'. Place the chart on a large table with the pasting materials.

What to do
Ask the children to sit in a circle. Talk about different hair colours using individual children as examples. Ask all of the children with black hair to sit in the centre. Encourage the children to count with you as you touch each child's head. Ask the children to return to their places. Repeat with blond hair, red hair and brown hair.

Individual task
Give each child a copy of the photocopiable sheet and ask them to use the outline on the sheet to draw and colour a picture of their own face and hair. Can they cut it out and paste it onto the chart in the correct box? Count together the number of faces in each box. Ask the children, 'Which set has the largest/smallest number of children?'. Discuss and compare the sets with the children.

Support
Help any children who have difficulty cutting out their face and pasting it onto the correct box on the chart.

Extension
Invite the children to look at the 'Hair colours' chart and ask some 'Let's pretend' questions such as, 'Let's pretend that one new child with brown hair has come to school today. How many faces would be in the brown hair box?', or 'Let's pretend that two children with blond hair are absent today…'.

Assessment
Check whether the child can describe the colour of her own hair and other children's. Can she count the total number of children in the group with each type of hair colour? Note whether she can compare two sets of different hair colours and say which has more or less.

Home links
Encourage parents and carers to sort sweets or biscuits into sets.

Hair today

Busy beading

Learning objectives
To count reliably up to ten or more beads; to write numerals up to 10 or more and draw the same number of items.

Group size
Four children working with an adult.

What you need
A copy of the photocopiable sheet for each child; large coloured beads in a tray; threading laces; a minute timer; large sheet of paper; flip chart; pencils; marker pen; crayons or felt-tipped pens.

Preparation
Make a score chart with the heading 'Bead threading scores' and three columns – 'Name', 'First turn', 'Second turn' – on a large sheet of paper. Attach it to the flip chart.

What to do
Explain to the children that they are going to thread beads onto a lace to see how many they can thread in one minute. Say, 'Ready, steady, go!' and start the timer.

Individual recording
Give each child a copy of the photocopiable sheet to draw and colour the beads that they have threaded onto the first lace. Ask them to count the beads and write the number in the

box underneath. Repeat the game filling in the second lace and box.

Write the children's names in the first column of the chart. Ask them in turn to write their first score in the 'First turn' column. Read out all the scores and ask the children who threaded the most beads. Ask that child to draw a circle around their score on the chart. For the 'Second turn', ask who threaded the smallest number of beads. Again, invite that child to draw a circle around their score on the chart.

Support
Let the children thread a necklace in their own time to wear for the remainder of the session.

Extension
Challenge the children to thread a necklace of more than 15 or 20 beads to wear for the remainder of the session.

Assessment
Check whether the child can thread a necklace and count the beads correctly. Note whether he can sort out and count the beads of one colour in a necklace of different-coloured beads.

Home links
Ask parents and carers to time how long it takes for their children to get undressed and ready for bed, and to write it down for their children to compare their times with other children's.

Busy beading

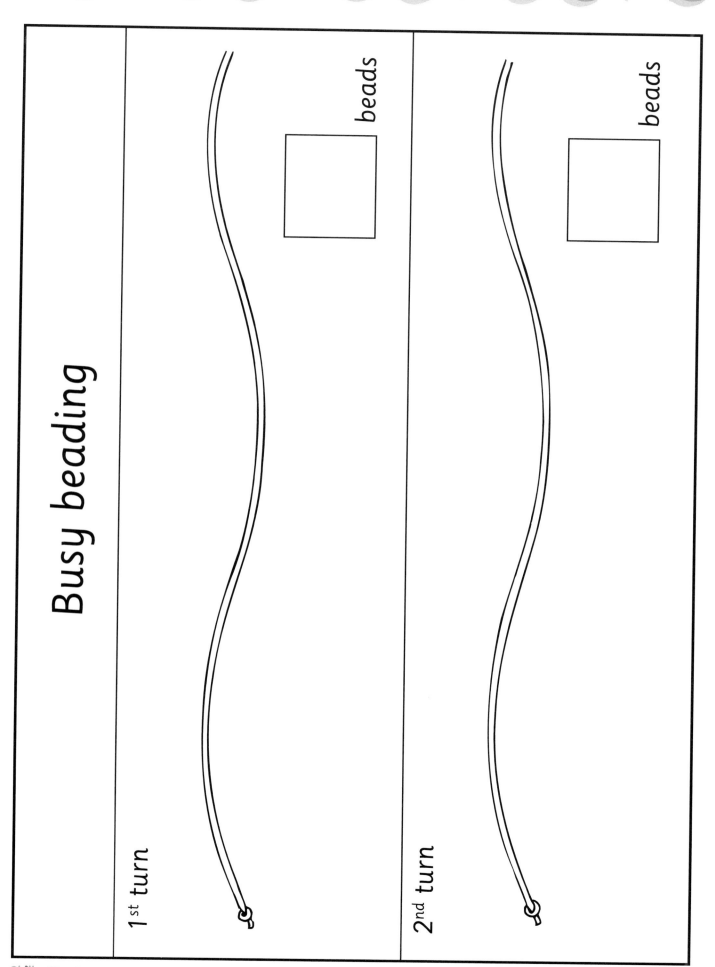

1st turn

beads

2nd turn

beads

Play time!

Learning objectives
To recognize numerals 1 to 12; to begin to use 'o'clock' when talking about time; to recognize the positions of hands on a clock showing times to the hour.

Group size
Four to six children working with an adult.

What you need
The photocopiable sheet; A3 card; scissors; flip chart; water-based marker pen; cleaning cloth.

Preparation
Enlarge two copies of the photocopiable sheet onto A3 card, laminate and cut up into individual time cards. Draw a large numbered clock-face without hands on a sheet of card. Mark the centre of the clock with a large spot and laminate. Attach the teaching clock to a flip chart and use with a water-based marker pen and a cleaning cloth.

What to do
Hold up the time cards in turn. Say the time on the card and then ask the children to say the 'o'clock' time together. Repeat until the children are familiar with the cards.

Play a version of the game 'What's the time, Mr Wolf?'. Choose a child to be Mr Wolf, shuffle the time cards and place the pile face down in front of Mr Wolf. The other children take turns to ask, 'What's the time, Mr Wolf?'. Mr Wolf shows a card to the group who say the time on it together. The game continues until Mr Wolf picks up the 12 o'clock card, when the children say loudly, 'Dinner time!'. A new Mr Wolf is chosen and the game starts again.

Individual task
Point to each number around the teaching clock and ask the children to say the numbers aloud. Using the water-based marker pen, draw the big hand pointing to the number 12. Tell the children that the big hand always points to the 12 at an o'clock time. Draw the small hand on the clock pointing to the number 2, and explain that when the little hand points to the number 2 on the clock, that tells us that it is two o'clock. Wipe off the small hand and draw it again, pointing to the number 5, saying, 'When the small hand points to the 5, the time is five o'clock'. Repeat this, drawing the small hand pointing to different numbers and asking the children to say the time in each instance. Spread the o'clock time cards out face up on the table. Draw the small hand pointing to a number on the clock and choose a child to say the time, then find the matching card on the table. Ask all the children to say the time. Repeat until all the cards have been used.

Support
Help the children to find time cards to match the time that you have drawn, by saying the time and directing them towards the correct card.

Extension
Ask the children to take turns to select a time card from the table, give the child the water-based marker pen and ask her to draw in the small hand on the clock to show the time.

Assessment
Note whether the child can recognize and say the names of o'clock times from the time cards. Note whether she can recognize and say the o'clock time drawn on the clock. Can she find a time card to match a time drawn on the clock?

Home links
Encourage parents and carers to use an old clock or watch to practise reading different o'clock times with their child.

Play time!

1 o'clock	2 o'clock	3 o'clock
4 o'clock	5 o'clock	6 o'clock
7 o'clock	8 o'clock	9 o'clock
10 o'clock	11 o'clock	12 o'clock

Name _____

Skills development chart

I can use simple measures, tools and counting to help me solve simple comparing and measuring problems.

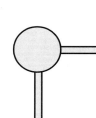

I can count up to ten or more objects.

I can compare two sets of objects and say if the sets have the same or different numbers of items.

I can compare two sets of objects and say which set has more or less items.

I can sort and compare numbers of objects that float or sink.

I can compare and order sets of three different-sized objects from largest to smallest.

I can compare two objects of different length and say which is the longer/ shorter object.

I can compare two objects of different weight/mass and say which is the heavier/lighter object.

Comparing

I can measure short distances by counting the number of paces to walk from one place to another.

I can count and say which distance was the nearest/furthest to walk to.

I can tell the time when a clock is showing an o'clock time.

I can measure the capacity of different-sized containers by counting the number of cupfuls of water to fill each container.

I can count and say which container holds the largest/smallest number of cupfuls of water.

I can balance an object with different sets of items and count the items.

I can count and say which set has the most/least items to balance an object.

Measuring